Satan! Guns! & Punk Rock!

A monologue by Wolf Larsen

Dedicated to Satan

ABOUT WOLF LARSEN

Wolf Larsen is a comedian, novelist, & playwright who has traveled to over 50 countries. For many years, Wolf worked as a seasonal laborer in Alaska. His work has been published in literary magazines around the world.

Other Books by Wolf Larsen

Capitalism Sucks! (non-fiction)

Pricks, Cunts, & Motherfuckers (a novel)

The Genital Herpes National Anthem (a novel)

Honky Fucking Crazy N-Word Lover (a novel)

Pornography (a book of poems)

Eulogy for the Human Race (a book of poems)

Shit! Fuck! Crap! (plays)

And there are many more books by Wolf Larsen to choose from.

The monologue begins:

"I lift my head off my body, and I throw my head up into the air... And my head lands in the middle of the audience. And my headless body jumps into the audience running around searching for my sanity, my sanity my sanity my sanity my sanity!

I paint my insanity all over the reader! I paint my music all over the walls of the city! And as the police chase me down the street, I scream out every obscenity known to man!

Because I am the most beautiful zombie that was ever born! I am the most pornographic heaven that has ever breathed! I am so much car crashes inside my head!

I am blessed with the nightmare of me! And so I paint my face over & over again all over the walls of this room! And all of my faces are screaming the words of this monologue!

I love you all like my feces! And I love my own feces! I pick my feces out of the toilet with my bare hands, and I smear my feces all over the walls of the bathroom! And that is why everyone loves me!

Everyone loves me because the sky is raining God's urine all over us! Because we are blessed with life, we are blessed with life because of our mother's sins! Our mother's sins with some handsome stranger poking her full of his herpes-filled penis! That is the afternoon of your conception! All of our conceptions are blessed with sin! And all of our sins are blessed with Wolf!

That's right! I bless all your sins! For I am the Priest of Sin! I love you all, the same way that I love the spermatozoa in my genitals! For how many of you are the sons & daughters of my sins? After all, I fucked 500 women! When your mother was bent over on all fours, I was fucking her like a horny dog, and then after I ejaculated you into your mother, your mother asked me to pee on her, and I did, and we both loved it!

Because peeing on people is like finding heaven! Peeing on people is like having anal sex with Elizabethan literature! Peeing on people is like so much fire everywhere! Peeing on people is poetry!

Did I mention that I went to high school with the great R Kelly? How's that for some name dropping?

But when my eyeballs are bouncing around, and the spermatozoa in my Balzac are all screaming: 'We're all on fire! The mushroom clouds are crawling all over our skin!' – Well, it's moments like that, when I feel the great circus of the world! It's all a crashing meteor of greatness!

That's why my feet talk to me of delirious love feasts! That's why my farts scream their royal pedigree to the world! Because the power of my farts is the power of destruction!

As you sit there in the audience, think of me as your lunatic President with his finger on the atomic button! Think of me as your Savior! Think of me as a circus clown!

And I hope you the audience & I will enjoy this evening of arson together! I hope that we will burn down your home together! I know that we will find ecstasy in the fires of joy together!

And these words will crash into your ears! These words will pollute your brains with this wonderful apocalypse! These words will incite your genitals to riot!

And that is why you must all love each other! You people in the audience must love each other with crazy rainbows! Feel a love of

splashing oceans for each other!

And now the tide of me & you is flooding forth!

My balls send their commands to my head, and

my head babbles it's wildfires out of my

mouth, and that all splashes onto the page!

From the page the words grow in huge vines

into the reader's ears! From the page the

words frolic & giggle into your ears! From the

page the words will rise into the sky!

And feel my exclamation points bashing into

your faces! I will masturbate with my words! I

will be a flash flood of screaming people

through all your minds! And my words will

grow cemeteries in all your minds!

After this monologue the walls of this performance space will never be the same! After the walls of this room have heard this monologue, the walls of this room will become eternal floods of madness! The walls of this room will become gateways into the imaginations of other species!

Because I am the Messiah of Butterflies! I am the Hoodlum of Heaven! I am the Savior of everything evil!

No one can be me! I cannot even be me! Because all the burning sky of me is on fire! Feel the drums in your veins! Feel the drums in these words! Feel the drums screaming throughout the world!

And the violins create a circus! And the saxophones of the world all create this monologue! And all the tubas of the world are right now creating a nymphomaniac-midget-orgy together!

Because I am the great conductor of all the world's music! Because I am the conductor of 200 nations across the world! I write an opera with 6000 human languages! The 6000 human languages percolating in my balls at this very moment!

And audience, what's percolating in your balls at this moment? What art is percolating in all the craziness of your balls?

And women, what Harlequin romance is growing in your pussy at this moment? What

Cubist architecture is dripping out of your pussy at this moment?

For I have made 500 pussies drip with the beginning of time! I have made 500 pussies have orgasms that splashed all the way into outer space! Because the fire in all our genitals is the fire of the gods!"

And now the saxophone player gets up and plays the fire of the gods. And the piano player plays 500 pussies dripping with the beginning of time. And the drums play orgasms splashing into outer space...

And the monologue man continues: "I was born in a convent of horny goddesses. I've always lived in a sideways-zigzagging-chaos. All my life I have felt that God's enormous penis would save the human race from boredom.

But now I am always being eaten by hungry gargoyles. And now I am searching for the 400 pound sex goddess that can quench my foot fetish. And now I will join all the talking lizards in my brains.

And you the audience will be my chicken soup. And the reader will be my giant lizard in French lingerie. And the human race will be billions of talking anuses.

For we are all rainbows in the imaginations of unicorns. We are all rodents walking on two legs.

And that's why the sky is always delicious. And that's why we're all manic machines of sex.

And that's why I love the thousands of highways in our brains."

The saxophone plays tons of highways in everybody's brains. And then the saxophone plays manic machines of assembly-line-sex. And now the saxophone is playing the delicious strawberry marshmallow of the sky.

The monologue man continues: "For we are all part of the music of billions of people! We are all swimming inside the imagination of a goldfish! And that's why the greatest philosophers in the world are the spermatozoa in our Balzacs!

My penis is the entrance to human civilization! My Penis is a god that rises up in triumph! And the pubic hairs growing out of my crotch are disciples of the true knowledge!

I love to kiss feet. I love to kiss the feet of the pretty ladies! Kissing the feet of the pretty ladies is a feast of delirious yearning! And that's why I'm the Grand Lizard of the Banquet of Sunshine!

If only I could kiss my own buttocks! It would be so wonderful to kiss my own buttocks! Because my buttocks are libraries of fleshy words! Because my buttocks are an exquisite landscape!

Everyone's buttocks is an exquisite landscape! And that's why we should worship our buttocks! That's right! We should worship our own buttocks! And we should worship the buttocks of others! We should do like the dogs, and smell each other's buttholes! That should be our greeting – smelling each other's buttholes!

If we smell each other's buttholes every day we will triumph! It will be a glorious triumph of butthole-smelling! And that's exactly what the human race needs!

You know what also the human race needs?! The human race needs spaceship-penises to explore the grand vagina of outer space! The human race needs new somewheres in outer space to go! And you all need thousands of nipples! I need thousands of nipples too!"

And the saxophone plays lots & lots of nipples! And the drums play words & brains playing hide-&-seek together! And the piano does an up through a bunch of down! And the female vocalist sings a thousand freight trains of skat!

And then the monologue man continues: "I am the day that you have always feared! A tomorrow empty of the human race is what I am! And I will forever be the King of the Imagination!

I see your eyes crawling upon me! Just as my eyes crawl upon all of you! Your ears eat my words! Your eyes eat my face! My eyes eat all your faces!

And this is the beauty of us together like this! Together, all of you & I are sharing a tornado of words! We're sharing my wife together!

So let's tear down this day! Let's tear down the sky! Let's tear down the universe!

I love you all! I told you, already, that I love each and every one of you! And that is why I want to eat all of you!

Because cannibalism is the answer! Because sex & cannibalism is always the answer! Sex & cannibalism is the delicious-vagina-pie in the center of the universe!

And that is why all of you love me! You all love me with all the emptiness inside of you! And I love you all like my favorite syphilis!

And I love the dogs & cats! They are delicious! And as I look at all of you, you all look delicious!"

The saxophone plays a delicious audience. And the female vocalist does more skat. Her voice doing skat sounds like assembly lines of beauty! Her voice doing stat sounds like Mount Everest melting into words!

And now the monologue man continues: "And that's why apples! And that's why we must become sculptures! We must all worship the endless schizophrenia!

Do you love me?! Of course you do! You the audience & I – we love each other! We love each other like outhouses painted with the tenderness of bright colors! And that is why animals love to be eaten! Have you ever heard of devouring the sunshine?!

And now let me speak to the readers. Hey reader, have you ever worshiped your own feet? Have you ever found yourself floating inside of some dog's brains?? Have you ever had a philosophical discussion with your own spermatozoa???"

The female vocalist does more skat. She sounds like so much shining moon. She sounds like diagonal voices slicing through everything. And the piano accompanies her. The piano sounds like the human race entangled in question marks. The piano sounds like the earth revolving & revolving around Alfred E Newman's head.

And now the monologue man continues: "Why are we devouring ourselves? Why are we flying like butterflies amongst the neon lights?? Why are we all doomed???

Why? Why?? Why???

Why is the chaos so delicious? And why is the up so crazy? And why is the ten-thousand-penis-monster so happy?"

The saxophone plays, and the saxophone plays the ten-thousand-penis-monster skipping happily down the street. And the saxophone plays delicious chaos.

And now the monologue man continues: "Roller skates! Yummy-sweaty-underwear! Banana penis WOW!"

And then the female vocalist does some skat. She sounds like the South Side of Chicago being eaten by a fish.

And the monologue man says: "Eat all my yesterdays! Bathe in all my eyeballs! Stick your hands into my dreams!"

And the drums say lots of naughty things. And the drums say happy nipples to all the nuns. And the drums say goodbye to the human race.

And the monologue man says: "I have space-alien-lust! My feet are swimming away from reality! Let's have sex with the dinosaurs!"

And the piano says lots of impossible things. And the piano says let's shit the music everywhere. And the piano says eat the Eiffel Tower.

And the monologue man says: "Tomorrow will be delicious with wars! I will paint my herpes all over Christianity! And the feminist nuns will save humanity from sex!"

And then there is a moment of silence...

And the female sings some skat. She sounds so sad that she's happy. She sounds as sad as the happiest of birds.

The monologue continues: "The streets jump into your head! All the octopuses are squirming & swimming around in your head! One thousand noises are banging & banging inside your head!

Because all your brains are a bunch of Gothic mazes! Your brains are squirming around the seven continents! Your brains are squirming around like an oversexed computer! Crashing brains! Festering brains!

And that's why dolphins are swimming around in God's Balzac! And the guns in our hands are a yellow-dandelion-logic! Isn't it interesting that the Americans that want gun control, are the same ones that want endless imperialist war? But anyway, have you ever scratched your brains out?! And what about the penises flying through the restaurants??

Because fucking smelly pussy is like talking about Aristotle with an orangutan! It's like strawberry fields growing all over our bodies!

And now the saxophone player will play smelly pussy for you!"

The saxophone player plays smelly pussy.

"You see audience, you see reader, the words are drunk with so much up! And that's why I have too many heads! That's why everybody in the audience is hallucinating me into existence! And that's why you should jump into the head of the person sitting beside you! You all should swim through each other's brains!

Because Tuesdays no longer exist! All Tuesdays have been replaced with mechanical-insanity-machines! Can't you see that maze-of-thoughts over there?! Can't you all see that big 'yes' flying through the air?!

We all must eat of the fruits of our sex! We all must defecate civilization everywhere every day! And the pigeons in the sky must understand philosophy! I tell the pigeons: 'You must write rainbows everywhere! You must paint your insanity all over the sky! You must howl & howl until everybody listens!'

But the pigeons never listen! The pigeons never listen to my wisdom!

Because my wisdom is a thousand doors opening-&-closing! My wisdom is an orgasm that lasts forever!

And what about your wisdom, audience/reader?! Is your wisdom about to explode?! Or is your wisdom about to grow daffodils?!

Because the world is going to explode! The world is going to explode with knowledge! The world is going to explode with dandelions!"

The saxophone plays the world exploding. The drums play the world exploding. And the piano is exploding with illegitimate children. And then the female vocalist, her voice begins to explode with lust.

And then the monologue continues: "Because I have ears that can hear the paintings! I am more Charles Manson than any pigeon in the sky! Can't you see my Cubist brains? Can't you see my visions flooding out of my eyes?

And as I stare at you the audience, and as I stare at all you readers through the page, I can see all of your World War 3! I can see all of your nightmares! That's right! I can see all of your sexy Garden of Edens frolicking through all your brains!

But never mind all that! Let's talk about subway trains traveling to the Italian Renaissance instead! Let's talk about our emotional thunderstorms instead!

Or maybe we should talk about the Washington monument as a porno sculpture?! Or perhaps, we should talk about having a grand tour of the Queen of England's 90-year-old vagina instead?! Or maybe we should just have sex with the pigeons in the park?!

Either way, the sky is allergic to us! Either way, the pornography of life will bless us with

God's holy jism! That's why I don't use deodorant!

When you the audience look at me, and when you readers see me on this page, do you see my herpes?? Do you see my eternal internal warfare?? Because I am not me! I am never me! I have always been somebody else! Are any of you yourselves?! None of you are yourselves! All of you are somebody else! Whether you realize it or not, you are all somebody else! None of you are yourselves!

But what about the fish swimming around these phrases of poetry? And what about all the doo-doo that I shitted on the street corner late last night? I wonder what the people thought when they were walking down the street this morning, and they saw human shit on the street corner, with used toilet paper??!!

Because that's my trademark! That's right, human shit with used toilet paper on the street corner, is my trademark! It's my beautiful me shining through! It's my manifesto!

And, I like to pee at the entrances of government buildings!

I also love to scream obscenities at the top of my lungs at all the dogs in the street! And when they bark at me, I bark at them right back!

I love to take off all my clothes on the subway, and scream mathematical equations at all the other passengers. And all the other passengers react to this with breakdancing. And some of them ask me: 'Where's heaven or the toilet?? I have to find the afterlife and take a shit!'

Because what is the jism of God?? I'm asking you the audience. I'm asking you the reader. I'm asking you: 'what is the syphilis & gonorrhea of liberty & justice for all??'

Isn't that why we're here today? Aren't we here today because of all the abstract expressionism painted with diarrhea & menstrual fluids & nuclear waste? Aren't we here today because of all the immaculate conception at Burger King?

But that's not why I'm here today! I'm here today because of all the leprechauns in my toaster oven! I'm here today because of all the basketball players fucking my wife!"

The saxophone player begins playing the NBA making immaculate conception with everybody's wives. But the piano player is playing something completely different. The piano player is playing a transvestite Beethoven sucking off all the big black Dicks of the NBA. Meanwhile, the female vocalist is singing a beautiful impressionistic Renoir painting. And the drums are lost between the brains of an insomniac, and the brains of everyone in the insane asylum.

The monologue continues: "And that's why puppy is so absolutely delicious! That's why urinating abstract expressionism all over the founding fathers of our country is so afternoon delight! And we should all urinate our abstract expressionism all over the founding fathers of our country! We should all float in the gravity-free environment of the Statue of Liberty's vagina!

Because of used toilet paper! Because of Martians in your soup!

Don't you all see the invisible Martians & gargoyles everywhere?? Because I can see all the Martians & gargoyles with my one-eyed penis! I can see all the black NBA players having a grand-old-orgy fucking all the founding fathers of our country up the ass! And I know all of you can see all that too!

Because all of us are ducks swimming in a pond the size of the universe! We are all Alfred E Newman on crack!

And there's nothing we can do about it!

Because everything is McDonald's hamburgers

with a side of World War 3 and a Coke!

Everything is flying around us in this capitalist

whorehouse we live in!

Nothing is as heavenly as hell! Nothing is as

Boing Boing as an apocalyptic penis! That's

right! Everything is right! Everything is wrong!

Everything is right & wrong with lots of

whoring virgins! Everything is left & right with

our buttocks turning into flying saucers!

Everything is up & down with photon torpedoes

shooting out of the eyes of Jesus Christ!

And that's why I masturbate all the time! And

that's why you all masturbate all the time! And

that's why everybody on this planet is

masturbating & masturbating & masturbating!

Can you see what I'm talking about?? Of

course you all can! You can all see me on stage

as a rooster riding a nuclear missile! And those

of you reading this can see me as the little

man on the page screaming flying cows at you!

I'm whispering 10,000 dancing naked Igor

Stravinsky clones to you all! And don't you

love me for it??

Don't you love me with lots of stabbing

knives?? And I know that you love my doo-doo

on the sidewalk every morning!

Let me tell you all something! Whenever I doo-

doo on the sidewalk in the middle of the night I

feel like the King of Gobbledygook! I feel like the King of Philosophy!

Why don't you all try it?? Why don't you all try doo-dooing on the sidewalk? Right after this play is done, why don't you all doo-doo on the sidewalk outside of this playhouse en masse?? And while you're all doo-dooing on the sidewalk in front of this playhouse, why don't you all scream?? Why don't you all scream whatever you feel like screaming?? It'll be an exercise in democracy! True democracy!

Hey! That gives me an idea! Why don't we all go to Washington DC together?? And why don't we all take a shit together on the steps of Capitol Hill? And then the next day, we can all take a shit together in front of the White

House! And then the day after that, we can all take a shit on the steps of the Supreme Court!

It'll be great! It'll be fantastic! It'll be 10,000 virgins crawling all around God's big black cock!"

And the saxophone starts to play the great fantastic big black cock of God in the sky. And the piano starts to play the great fantastic big black cock in heaven. And the female vocalist begins to sing the great fantastic pussy-eating-feast in heaven.

The monologue continues: "Today I got off the bus at the Eternal Nipple Factory in Heaven. Then the street corner did a loop around craziness! Everybody on the street corner was doing harmonious-racial-relations-up-the-nose together.

A lady jumped out of a giraffe's butt, and told me: 'You've got to burn down everybody's personalities! And then we're going to build new personalities out of everywhere in the universe! And after that we're going to party in hell!'

I responded to her: 'Look, you sunshine lady that jumped out of a giraffe's butt! I only have sex with midgets on the planet of Pluto! And sometimes an occasional sheep!"

Then a subway train flew out of the lady's vagina, and crashed into everything!

So then I became a giraffe. Then the lady jumped out of *my* butt. That's when the lady says to the reader: 'Mars is the best planet for orgies! There you will find lots of bootylicious!'

And then the audience says to the reader: 'You should be eating these words fried up with salt & catchup & grilled onions!'

And the reader YELLS at the audience: 'I already had sex with all the space aliens of the universe today!!'

But nobody hears the reader, because time has been stolen by somebody. Time no longer exists.

This causes everyone on the planet to be infected by Wolf Larsen's brains. And now giraffes are jumping out of everybody's butts everywhere! The United States Air Force had been preparing for this for quite some time, so the United States Air Force all dress up as women, and have sex with the neo-czar of Russia.

Meanwhile, the President of the United States has turned into a dinosaur. So somebody is selected at random from the audience to become President of the United States of America.

The new President of the United States of America turns out to be even crazier than the last President. The new President orders everyone to eat their own doo-doo in order to encourage recycling. And the new President of the USA also orders lots of cocaine for everybody!

So all the animals in zoos across the world escape, and they begin writing strange-new-words on all the streets across the planet."

The saxophone plays zoo animals rioting on streets across the planet. Meanwhile, the piano is playing Mozart being fucked up the ass by Wolf Larsen. The female vocalist is doing a sexy Ferris wheel with her voice. And the drums are playing a fun-filled vacation full of lots of genocide!

The monologue continues: "That's when I decided to go snorkeling in the sky. While I was snorkeling I saw lots of dead people floating everywhere... All of the sudden, all the audience members were snorkeling in the sky with me. Some of the audience members were eaten by nerdy millennials.

Then the readers of this monologue all parachuted out of Satan's butt. And all the readers ended up landing in heaven. This is when John Wayne Gacy of the Martian Rolling Stones sang: 'Eating your fellow human being is like too much WOW! It's like bullets flying everywhere making a symphony together!'

Mick Jagger was busy that day doing drugs with Attila the Hun. Of course, a Tyrannosaurus Rex jumped out of the butt of Attila the Hun! And this is why I have testicles!

Now, lots of fornicating rabbits! You see??

Right now, I'm seeing Charles Manson & Jesus Christ running on the Republican presidential ticket together! Are you all seeing Charles Manson & Jesus Christ in the White House together?? And this is why we should all hallucinate new religions together!

Together, the audience, the reader, the writer, & myself the performer – together we are all a giant painting of a nervous breakdown! Together we are all lots of artsy-fartsy pornographic videos! And that's why I'm running for President with Hunter Thompson as Vice President on the Democratic ticket, against the Republican ticket of Charles Manson & Jesus Christ!"

The drums start to play lots of brightly-colored-sexy-polkadots. The female vocalist is flying around a sexy orgy of words.

The monologue man continues: "Anyway, as I was saying, the solar system is made out of doggy brains! And that's why I chopped up somebody on the bus today, and ate them. They asked me to eat them. And they tasted like the turn-of-the-century with strawberries. Did I eat them out with my tongue? Or did I eat them with a knife & fork? You decide! I think that the readers & the audience members should all eat each other!

Anyway, right now, all your dogs & cats are thinking: 'Let's eat our owners! Let's dance to the moon going around & around the earth!'

And I can read the minds of all the audience members. You're all thinking: 'Our brains are going to start walking in different directions!

We better take all our clothes off now! We all better start having sex with as many space aliens as we can find!'

And the readers are all thinking: 'This monologue is swallowing me! And I want to be swallowed! Please swallow me!!'

And that is why New York City is made out of verbs!"

The piano starts playing 15 million New Yorkers all having a nervous breakdown together. The female vocalist is singing her own nervous breakdown with the piano.

The monologue man continues: "Now, say that you have a nuclear missile up your butt. Or, maybe you were born on the moon of a different planet. At any rate, the millions of planets & moons in this monologue are delicious! And that is why I have herpes!

But, if you subtract herpes from the Republican Party, and you add a bunch of seasoning like garlic & pepper, and then you multiply that by a nuclear war, what do you get?? You get a bunch of naked Siamese twins dancing out of this monologue! That's what you get!

And that's why I ate your cat for breakfast."

The saxophone starts playing delicious fried cat with grilled onions.

The monologue man continues: "What I don't understand is why sunshine with gunshots is so delicious! Do you understand why a penis with ice cream & cherries is so delicious??

And that's why we need sex robots from the Italian Renaissance! Or do we need lots of herpes parachuting out of the sky??

Actually, what we really need is a decapitated human head for dinner! Because lots of abstract expressionism is cumming with your fried chicken dinner! And what should be our response?? Should we respond with painting our menstrual fluids all over a canvas, and hanging it up in an art museum? Or should we respond by jumping into a thousand different universes and never coming back? Or should we masturbate until a thousand Richard Nixon clones in French lingerie show up at our front door?

Only the jury of drug addicts can decide. The jury of drug addicts must decide if all the penises sticking out of God's face are a religious revelation or an hallucination! And they must also decide if there is intelligent life on earth! Otherwise, Charles Manson's thoughts will start floating everywhere! You see??

Of course you see! You see the hallucinations piling up on the doorstep! You see the crack-cocaine rainbows flying around the planet Earth! You know you do! That's why you pooh-pooh!

Because pooh-pooh is like thousands of talking elephants showing up at your doorstep! Pooh-pooh is like lots of verbs in your brains! And that's why all my hallucinations & sexual fantasies are politically correct! They are as politically correct as everyone bending over and smelling each other's buttocks at a cocktail party. We can learn a lot from dogs!"

The female vocalist sings a dog being eaten by its owner.

The monologue man continues: "Too many fish swimming out of your mouth?? Yes! Or is it no? Or maybe, everyone sharing their wives with German shepherds is fun?

Of course, fried verbs with spicy nouns is delicious with lots of sex! And maybe the Mafia is happy to see you! And maybe the sexy feet of a gorilla in the zoo is the answer! That's why eyeballs are delicious!"

The saxophone plays delicious eyeballs.

The monologue continues: "Delicious eyeballs! Delicious eyeballs! Delicious eyeballs! And that's why I worship my herpes as a religion! And when you ride a nuclear submarine into your wet dreams, cannabis happens! And when you're flying around & around a windmill in outer space, schizophrenia happens! Yes!

Yes to schizophrenia! Yes to the rats in the subway eating us! Yes to the streets running off to fairytales!

And hallelujah too! Hallelujah to all the whores in the whorehouses! Hallelujah to all the jackhammers flying everywhere! And hallelujah to all the motorcycles zooming off into your fantasies!

I jack off all the time with my hallelujah!"

The saxophone plays jacking off with your hallelujah...

The monologue continues: "Because jacking off with your hallelujah is like loopy brains for dessert! It's like going for a stroll in somebody else's wet dreams! It's like car crashes & more car crashes & more car crashes!

Hey audience! Hey reader! How often do you jack off with your hallelujah! Your right hand & your penis making glory hallelujah together! My right hand & my penis have made glory hallelujah together somewhere between 40,000 to 60,000 times! Think of all those orgasms! Think of all those spermatozoa swimming off into all those vaginas in the convent! It's so much immaculate conception with the right hand!

That's why I say glory hallelujah with lots of jizz! And lots of jizz with lots of capitalist political speeches! And lots of capitalist political speeches with lots of dancing-shaking-big-buttocks! And lots of dancing-shaking-big-buttocks with lots of preachers preaching the hallelujah! And lots of preachers preaching the hallelujah with lots of family values bouncing around in our Balzacs..."

The saxophone plays lots of family values bouncing around our Balzacs...

The monologue continues: "And that's why I always grow pubic hairs all over the moon! And that's why you should all grow pubic hairs all

over the moon! Because devouring comets &
asteroids for breakfast is great! Wouldn't it be
great if everybody in the audience – and all the
readers of this book – were all to start making
glory hallelujah with their right hands &
penises right now??

So sex robots doing the mushroom clouds in a
pornographic video! And anyway, asteroids &
comets are always best served with delicious
puppy! That's right! That's right to all the
poppy fields growing across the universe!
That's wrong to all the oceans of humanity in
our balls! Right?

But what about the wild desires in our eyes?
And what about the violence & sex dripping
everywhere? And I just don't know about all

the power-hungry capitalist psychopaths running the 200 nations on earth!

And that's why I hired Sam the Silly. Sam the Silly is always there for me. He's always there for me when I have to take a shit into the brains of the audience! He's always there for me whenever I have to pee my words all over humanity!"

The female vocalist sings the praises of Sam the Silly...

And then the monologue continues: "I wish I was more insane than a normal person! And then I turn back into a frog again! And after that I have sex with all the words in this monologue! Hey! Are all you guys going to have sex with all the words in this monologue?

Are you sure? Are you sure about all the people floating everywhere??

Because tomorrow is coming! And what if tomorrow is full of lots of talking-dead-people?? And what if tomorrow the massive-orange-suicide happens?? And what if tomorrow all the planets of the universe fall on your house??

What will all the lizards in your toilet do?? Will all the lizards in your toilet think?? Or will they eat each other's brains?

All I know is that human heads are floating everywhere! You know what I mean?? Of course you all know what I mean!! You all know, just like I know, that yesterday keeps happening over & over again! You all know, just like I know, that the sky is delicious with spicy verbs!

And that's why my reality is full of maggots devouring everything! Is your reality full of maggots devouring everything?? If not, then you should marry a manikin at the department store at once! And then you should travel into your dreams! And after that, you all should masturbate each other for the next thousand years!

Because lots of pineapples! And that's why the wolves are all jumping out of our scrambled eggs!"

The drums start to play a bunch of wolves jumping out of our scrambled eggs with lots of energy.

The monologue continues: "I have too many heads for all the spermatozoa! The music makes me become another person! And that's when I have to masturbate all the animals in the zoo with my magical hands!

But, our own children will eat us! And who really knows if sanity isn't just a socially-acceptable form of insanity! And that's why huge skidale-do-bop all the time! You see what I mean?? Because if the huge skidale-do-bop is fresh, then happy hookers for everybody! And we'll be saved! We'll be saved by Jesus Christ doing the cha-cha-cha! And then the Devil will save our dogs & cats with his mighty erection! You see??

I can see the mighty erections of all the nuns in the bordellos! Can you see the mighty erections of all the nuns in the bordellos?? Can you? Can you?? Because if you can't see the mighty erections of all the nuns in the bordellos, then the monologue will collapse all over society!

And now it's time for too much delicious! Let's all dance with death! And we can sing together! We can sing the glorious road to death together!"

The female vocalist sings the glorious road to death. The drummer accompanies her with lots of bashing-&-crashing across the Middle Ages. And then the piano jumps in with lots of bright & dark colors splashing everywhere. And the saxophone is off in a creative universe playing some Hieronymus Bosch.

The monologue man continues: "And that's why it's time for Hieronymus Bosch & Pablo Picasso to dance together! And it's time for so much midnight! And it's time for suspicion to jump out of every street corner!

Because gunshots are delirious! So much words to eat! Too much scrambled thoughts cooking in the frying pan of your brains!

But not enough everywhere for everybody! And where's the everywhere?? What happened to it?? Did one of you eat the everywhere with lots of insanity sauce all over it??

And how about some cuu cuu sauce all over this monologue?! And I love all of the boing-

boing-boing in my ears! My mouth is really a spaceship of words! And my dog is a spy for the CIA! My cat, my cat is a terrorist with evil plans! My cat loves to play with space satellites all night long!

And my wife?? My wife lives on another planet! My wife is a robot with thousands of gears constantly moving! What is your wife? Is your wife a madman with a pair of tits & a vagina??

And women, what about your husbands? Are your husbands all computers?? Or are your husbands a zigzagging crazy of too many different personalities – all in five minutes??

And what about the children?? What about your children, audience? Did you eat your children before you came here??

What an interesting audience! I bet you're all a bunch of tornadoes! Or maybe you're all a bunch of robots spying on behalf of the dogs & cats!

And what about the readers of this here monologue? They're holding this monologue in their hands as a book – all these readers – and all these readers are thinking as they're reading. What are the readers thinking?? Are the readers thinking: 'sex with animals is all right by me'? Or are the readers thinking: 'we must build buildings out of everything crazy soaring up into the sky'?

You know what I'm thinking? I'm thinking that everybody on this planet wants to eat me! No I'm not! I'm thinking that we must mix poetry

& architecture with our cum juices! No I'm not!
Yes I am! No I'm not! Yes I am!

No I'm not a communist space alien smoking
lots of poetry all day long! Yes I am a
communist space alien smoking lots of poetry!

Yes I am a bird that flies around all the giant
testicles floating in outer space! No I'm not a
bird! I'm really a zombie! I'm a zombie that ate
its way out of Leonardo da Vinci's brains! And
here I am – talking to you!

No, I'm not a painting that's been inside your
brains for centuries! Yes I am a painting! I
don't really exist!

I tell you what! I'll let all of you readers &
audience decide! For all of you that believe
that I have the sexiest feet you've ever seen,

then you should fly to the moon to indicate

yes! But if you think no, then you should fly to

the Last Supper of Jesus Christ instead! Or

maybe you should skip-skip-skip da-de-do!

Skip-skip-skip da-de-do! Skip-skip-skip da-de-

do all the way to Heaven & Hell!

And how many of you believe that I am a

zombie from the Balzac of some cannibal?? All

of you that believe I am a big human dildo,

should dance with each other right now! Or

perhaps you should pee all over each other

instead! Or maybe you should jump into a

1970s telephone and never come back??

But what were we talking about?? Oh yeah, we

were talking about eating zombies for

breakfast. No, wait! We were talking about

something else. Oh, I know! We were talking about wandering around in the empty ruins of the world 100 years from now! No?!?

Well, why don't we talk about sticking pink unicorns up our butts?!? Or maybe we should talk about giant space stations growing out of our ears?!? Or how about painting music all over each other's derrières?!?

And what happened to all the thousands of Eiffel Towers in your scrambled brains?!? Ha ha ha ha ha ha ha ha aha ha ha ha ha!!!"

Then the monologue man starts crying. As he sobs, the monologue man says: "There's just too many happy people in the cemetery! And that's why I always wash myself with bright colors! Back when I was a waiter, I used to spit my poetry into everybody's food! I did good? Yes??"

The monologue man continues sobbing, as the female vocalist does thousands of years of sobbing with her voice. The saxophone does a thousand years of laughing all around her voice.

Then the monologue man starts dancing erratically as he shouts: "Mustard!! Used condoms!! Hot Diggity dog!!"

The saxophone plays a frenzied hot Diggity dog with lots of used condoms!

And the monologue man continues dancing erratically as he's shouting: "Bourgeois pigs delicious!! Sexy sex robot toes to kiss all day!! Nuclear Armageddon tomorrow?!!"

And now, the female vocalist sings a frenzied nuclear Armageddon!

And the monologue man makes erratic movements as he shouts: "Please kill me with Stravinsky!! I want to give you all the Greek gods in my Balzac swimming inside of you!! Richard Jackass Daley!!"

And now the piano starts to play Greek gods swimming in everybody's Balzacs...

And the monologue man holds still. And he whispers: "Hand grenades! Get drunk with me! Let's drink all of Igor Stravinsky's symphonies together!"

And now the piano is playing a violent-chaotic-everything!

And the monologue man says in an up-&-down crazy voice: "Eat me with lots of happiness! Stick all my words up your butt! Let's kiss each other's buttocks with lots of nuclear power!

This is where the buildings are eaten by music. This is where I eat all the insanity in the mental wards. Then the sky welcomes us with open arms. And we swim up the sky. We swim up into the big mouse turd of the sky!

But what vacation of psychotic pubic hairs is this? What lunatic with the atomic button is in the White House now? That is the question. The question is so upside down!

And what is the answer?? The answer is lots of masturbating! The answer is all of us sailing into poetry together!

But what about swimming up into the sky?? Up in the sky there's lots of horny devils. Up in the sky there's lots of dead people!

God's pubic hairs will provide for us all! The anus of Jesus Christ will give us lots of food. And the breasts of the holy Virgin Mary will deliver lots of vodka to our lips.

Lots of vodka! Lots of angry birds devouring all our thoughts!

But what about anal sex with all the penguins in Antarctica? And what about all of us walking to the beginning of time together?

Do you ever think about these things? What does your brain do? Does your brain somersault & somersault around & around the world again & again?? Do you ever think about chopping up your neighbor's dog and cooking it, and then serving your neighbor's dog to your neighbor??

Anyway, heaven is where the dead people all party together! Heaven is where there's rivers of cocaine instead of rivers of water. And heaven is where giant vaginas jump out of dark alleyways and attack you!

And that's why I love the snails crawling along the 19th century... That's why I love the way we stab each other all night long... I love the way the mushroom clouds look in your eyes!

What do you all love?? Do you love the crackheads when they beg to be eaten alive?? Do you love the taste of human flesh as much as I do??

That is the question. There are no answers.

There are a million answers."

The saxophone plays a million answers. And

the female vocalist sings the song of no

answers...

"So how long will the human race be here??

After 200,000 years existing as Homo sapiens

we may be extinct soon. Nuclear war. Artificial

intelligence. Those damn scientists beaming

our existence to the space aliens in outer

space, so that they can come here and eat us.

What will we taste like to the space aliens??

Will we taste like Shakespeare?? Or will we

taste like a hot dog??

And what if our dogs & cats could chop us up

and eat us?? Would we taste like poetry to our

dogs & cats?? Or would we taste like God's 10 Commandments to our precious dogs & cats??

When you go home tonight why not ask your dog or cat if they would like to eat you? And if you're reading this book at home, why not ask your dog or cat to pee on you? Why not??

Why not get drunk with the Devil for the next thousand years?? Why not be saved by Jesus farting his extraterrestrial boobylicious all over us??"

The saxophone player plays dancing-space-aliens doing the polka with lots of horny dogs. And the female vocalist sings lots of horny songs in all the space alien languages.

The monologue man continues: "But what have we discovered here?? Have we discovered

the knowledge & philosophy inside of a
German shepherd's hairy balls?? Have we
discovered the ocean between our ears??

We have discovered Salvador Dali swallowing
the Theory of Relativity out of Albert Einstein's
big black dick! Yes! That's it! And we've also
discovered the sun exploding a beautiful
summer day all over us!

You understand??

You understand the delicious psychopath
recipe of this monologue??

But what about tomorrow?? Will tomorrow be
made out of elephant farts?? Will the planet
earth be invaded by outerspace poetry
tomorrow?

I'm curious! I'm curious about all the delicious-spicy-pussy! And I'm curious about all the Albert Einstein erections at my favorite restaurant!

Are you curious about all the Albert Einstein erections at your favorite restaurant?

The only answer is to create a religion of Sexy Feet Worship! Or is the answer painting our diarrhea all over the United States Congress?

And that is why lots of cockroaches love you! Lots of butterflies absolutely love you all with lots of butterfly love! And that's why hemorrhoids are a great source of wisdom!

Can you see the space aliens scratching their booty holes with outer space hemorrhoids? Can you hear the hemorrhoids in your booty hole discussing philosophy with each other? Can

you smell the nouns & verbs burning

everywhere? Can you touch the laughter?

And that's why we need Massive Tickling

Ceremonies in Tickling Temples built especially

for The Annual Tickling Fest! We need Cubism

& Impressionism & fauvism in our food!

I was eating my food, for example. And my

food tasted like Pierre Renoir. It did! And then

the food on my plate told me: 'Jump on top of

the table in this crowded restaurant and rip off

your clothes and scream obscenities at the top

of your lungs!'

And I responded to the food on my plate:

'Look, man, I'm from Brooklyn!'

Because Harry Krishna Harry Krishna Harry Krishna! Because my herpes sores love this audience!

Why else would the reader of this monologue suddenly run out into the streets absolutely naked?? You see??

And that's why Igor Stravinsky is the greatest! And I haven't even eaten myself yet! You know, I taste like the Iraq War even though I've never been to Iraq! So I eat myself every day!

Do you eat yourself every day?? Do you smoke a bowl of religion in the crackhouse?? Or do you inject all the stories of the Old Testament into your veins with a needle??

Well, do you? Do you?

Well, I'm afraid that the pigeons flying around the plaza are going to steal my penis! And I'm also afraid that this monologue is going to give me a 500 year long erection!

It's a fear made out of music!

But I'm also happy! I'm happy with painting endless nipples all over my walls! I'm happy with vomiting all my wars into the toilet after I eat!

But I'm also sad! I'm sad with smiling clowns jumping out of my penis! I'm sad with feet that want to go everywhere but can't!

Are you all sad with 10,000 volcanoes in the mirror?? Hey you – reader – are you happy & sad with the cemetery calling you?

And you – the audience – are you happy & sad with your life crashing into thousands of different directions?

I'm happy & sad with waves of humanity drowning me! But only on yesterdays!

What about you, audience & readers? Are you happy & sad with all your yesterdays drowning you?"

The entire band plays happy & sad with lots of yesterdays drowning everybody...

Monologue man continues: "I try to find myself. But I find myself swallowing whole cities! And then I find myself erupting in so many different directions!

Hey readers & audience: you ever find yourself erupting in so many different directions?? You ever find yourself sailing across a sea of black people??

It's the stormy weather of humanity silently screaming at you wherever you go! It's the crashing meteors around our daily lives! It's all the criticizing eyes putting a noose around our necks every day!

And that's why the paintings splash a million colors of darkness at me!

I drink the thunderstorms! I eat the diseases! I snort the smiles of the children up my nose! I smoke religion with a lighter at all hours of the day & night.

And whenever I smoke religion with a lighter –
magical-washing-machines happens! And then
the beginning & the ending of the human race
happens! And then after that, it's a great big
orgy between heaven & hell!

Is that what happens to you all when you
smoke that religion??"

The entire band plays smoking that religion...

The monologue man continues: "Which brings
up the question – why not burn down the
planet Earth?? And that brings up another
question, why is destruction so beautiful? And
why is the human race on fire?

Do you know the answer to that, readers &
audience? Do you know the answer to
grinding-intergalactic-machines devouring

whole planets? And do you know the answer to midnight when monsters leap out of God's penis in heaven, and descend onto the planet Earth to fornicate us?"

The saxophone plays all the answers to God's mysterious penis in heaven. And the female vocalist sings all the answers to grinding-intergalactic-machines devouring all the planets.

And the monologue man continues: "And what is it about all our yesterdays? Do all our yesterdays pile up like a bunch of decapitated human heads? And what about our today? Is our today a great big sunny sky squirting blue orgasms all over us?

But I have a question for you all: what is the answer to a dead body next to you in bed in the morning, and you don't know how it got there, or who this person is?? And I have another question for you all: what is the correct way to get to Alice in Wonderland's vagina? And what is this mysterious face that you're all giving me??

If any of you know the answers to these questions, please take your clothes off right now! And then ride a big flying vibrator all the way to the moon! Because I love a big space alien Dick in my butt!

And that's the answer! That's the answer to Salvador Dali's art! Or is it the answer to flushing the American nation down the toilet?

Or was that the answer to hopping on a hopping hopper machine all the way to the Hopping Olympics? But what was the question? Was the question about the crazy-crazy of the crazy-crazy-crazy? Or maybe we should provide all the answers, before we come up with the questions!

Because that's the way you drink the royal jizz of English aristocracy!"

The drums play the Royal jizz of English aristocracy swimming up the red carpet to a heaven full of dogs' brains. The piano plays lots & lots of questions. And the female vocalist is singing a thousand childhoods splashing everywhere...

And the monologue continues: "Because that's the answer to a strange man in a raincoat flashing you! You see?? All the birds in the sky see! The trees can see too! The trees have eyes! The trees can see all of the thoughts in the birds' heads! Can you see all of the thoughts in the birds' heads??

And that's why Salvador Dali's boogers taste like summer kissing winter! And that's why the planet Earth is a big booger in a goat's imagination! And what about the sun god & the moon god having extramarital sex?? And what about all the monkeys jumping around in our heads??

This is why I always wipe my ass with the faces of capitalist politicians! Do you all wipe

your ass with the faces of capitalist politicians?
Because outerspace with lots of pussy juices
oozing all over the night sky! The night sky is
very happy with lots of orgasms!

That is my reason for existing! Is the night sky
dripping with happy orgasms your reason for
existing? Because with naked well-hung
leprechauns running everywhere we can
always call up the planet Saturn! Yes? No? No
100 story skyscrapers to have anal sex with?
Is all the faces of the audience staring wildly at
me a yes? Or is all the faces staring silently at
me a no?

Sexy mermaids swimming around the
mushroom clouds is both no and yes! Yes?
Interstate highways flying off into

Shakespeare's plays – yes? Or giant dildos with wings flying off into space alien vaginas – no?

With drunken Shakespeare clones we can always party! Party with naked Shakespeare clones laughing as they're being whipped by dominatrix English teachers! This nightclub of S & M is so very up & down! Even sideways with lots of Boing Boing! Which is why the Boing Boing is always cooked medium-rare... With lots of decapitated human heads on the side!

Now look in your brooding silence! Is the dead body of Jimmy Hoffa in there? Because barking question marks is so very English! Or is it so very French? And lots of lunging lunacy is so very Spanish! So very very Spanish that

lunging lunacy! Especially when you add a
bunch of spices & babbling intellectuals! And
with all the babbling intellectuals we can
always conquer the Babylon of Endless Babble!
Do you feel dipper-clanky-boozy today?

Does the thunder & lightning jumping out of all
the vaginas in heaven make you feel high-
voltage?"

The saxophone plays thunder & lightning
jumping out of all the vaginas in heaven. But
the piano is playing lots of ringing telephones.
And the drums are playing a different kind of
PLOP-SICK-perversity.

The monologue continues: "You searching for a
gulping washing-machine on two legs? Because
that's the –"

All of a sudden the female vocalist begins singing an adjective that's hitting you upside the head. And the drums jump in with an exorcism. And the piano is doing a tiptoe through madness...

Then the monologue continues: "Inhaling all the craziness? Precious hours of masturbating to the space satellites revolving & revolving around the planet Earth? Lots of psychopathic flavors at the Crazy Man's Ice Cream Shoppe? Let's all jump into the computer and become space aliens!

Because the why & the who & the when & the how is also very dangling! It's also very gunshots with happy adjectives! Because crazy corkscrews uncorking the planet Earth, no? Or yes? Your personality sinking into thousands of voids? A yes of hilarious comedy to snort up our noses?"

The female vocalist sings yes and more yes and more yes! And the saxophone is singing a sexy yes and more sexy yes and more sexy yes. The piano is playing his own very sexy yes-yes-yes!

The monologue continues: "So yes-yes-yes is the canvas we're painting! And the canvas we're painting is the yes-yes-yes! Yes!

Words rushing out of the dictionary at you! Words rushing out of our minds and filling the air with imaginary images flowing & flying around us! And playing basketball with the decapitated heads of your enemies is so very acoustical! And this crack-cocaine-accordion music is so very what? What is the Devil's music without the Devil Worship in the Temple of the Devil? The Temple of the Devil is in my glorious mind! Is Hell everywhere on the immensity of the earth?? Or is hell only a glorious place in my fantasies?"

The saxophone plays a thousand sexual fantasies...

The monologue continues: "Because Satan is so very perpetual rebellion! Perpetual rebellion is why I'm cooking up these words with Satanic joy! And live bullets in the casserole is the reason why – hey, audience! – What is the reason for flying to Paris to fuck the Mona Lisa in the Louvre? Huh?? Huh?!

Hey audience! Answer me with a rhapsody! Or answer me with lots of screams!

Hey reader! Answer me with a vibrating vibrator vibrating the liberal/conservative blah-blah-blah vibrating out of the mouths of politician-vibrators! Or answer me with lots of horniness!"

The drums play a very violent storm of horniness. The female vocalist sings a very festive Festival of Horniness.

The monologue continues: "And sometimes that leads to pregnant virgins! Or it leads to peppermint abortions! Or maybe it leads to nudism? Nudism is the reason for the Nudist Monarchy of the planet Earth? Or is it the reason for the grandeur of our buttocks??

Anyway, big fracas! Big fracas is so very... So

very... So very... INCUUUUUUMING!"

The saxophone plays INCUUUUUUMING!...

The monologue continues:

"INCUUUUUUMING!! Yes! So much yes! Sunny

days with yes! Considerable diarrhea with

more yes! And buzzing vibrator-politician-

mouths with even more yes!

Because yes is the blinking-blinking-spaceship-

vibrators of outer space! And festive Beastiality

Festivals is also lots of yes! Yes to the echoing

orgasm machine! Because the orgasm machine

of tomorrow is the way to yes! And the way to

yes is the way to immediate sunflowers smiling

everywhere!"

The piano plays a way to sunflowers smiling everywhere...

The monologue continues: "The way to the Heavenly Kingdom of Running Around Naked is here! It's so jumping-crazy-teenagers! It's so very very farewell to tradition! Everything is so very very tomorrow with lots of new! So very very get drunk on sex robot jizz!"

The drums play some so very very drunk on sex robot jizz.

The monologue continues: "Yesterday some very very hooligan-erupting-art happened! And after that, some fantastic fantastic happened! And then some faraway happened too! And you know what happened after that?? The audience converted to a thousand different religions that they made up on the spot!

And once the audience converted to all these religions of sex & nudity, then... Then... Then... buzzing-buzzing-buzzing happened! And now? And now?"

The saxophone plays and now? And now?

The monologue continues: "And now the big grotesque civilization of Christianity will become a new hell! And then the new now will become a dark cave where billions of people are moaning in ecstasy! And the universe devouring us will be the very now! It will be so very now that a big celebration is due! A Celebration of Ecstasy!

And then... And then... And then..."

The saxophone plays a bunch of and then...
And then... And then...

The monologue continues: "And then lots of jiggling -jiggling-jiggles! And after that, lots of jiggling buildings doing the earthquake dance! And then lots & lots of jiggling boobs on the evening news!

Can you feel my yesterdays? Can you feel my tomorrows? Can you feel all the venereal diseases of my today?

Because my today is so very splattering-about-everywhere! My today is so much more prowling than my yesterday. And my tomorrow already happened! Yes! My tomorrow already happened in my wet dreams!

What about your wet dreams reader?

What about your wet dreams audience??

Wet dreams and more wet dreams and more wet dreams and more wet dreams!"

The saxophone plays wet dreams and more wet dreams and more wet dreams and more wet dreams...

The monologue continues: "Because I'm walking around in this maze of wet dreams! Wet dreams is the new destination we're all flying off to!

So have some intergalactic sex with your breakfast, audience! And have some madness sprawling throughout the city, reader!

That's why I have lots of splendid unicorns with my tipsy Saturday nights! That's why I have lots of feet with my zippers! All my scrambled brains are contagious!

Hey reader! Hey audience! Are you all contagious? Are you contagious with lots of yesterdays crawling all over you? Or are you contagious with too many eyeballs?"

The saxophone plays something so contagious that birds begin falling out of the sky. And the drums are playing so contagious that the continent of Antarctica crashes into the monologue.

The monologue continues: "Everything's contagious with your nightmares growing everywhere! Is it like billions of automobile tires rolling off the planet Earth and into outer space? I'm not sure! I'm not sure about anything, except that all these cartoon characters in my brains are screaming all the time! And that's absolutely true! It's absolutely true that night crawlers are in these words! Or otherwise, the radios in your brains would blow up, no? And why else?

And why else the ludicrous cackle?

And right now I'm lost! I'm lost in the middle of your intelligence! I'm lost in the middle of this tornado! And eternity keeps attacking me! And courteous killing is the only salvation!

It's the salvation of symphonies of naughty body parts! It's the salvation of verbs shooting through the air! It's the salvation of silliness!"

The saxophone plays the Salvation of Silliness. The piano plays the Salvation of God's Sins.

The drums play the Salvation of Naughty Body Parts...

The monologue continues: "That's why, only giant lizards devouring us can save us from the sunshine! But what about the refugees from the insanity of insanity land? And the spreading virus of normality is very scary!

And you know what's also scary? Medieval monks with giant penises floating through the land of make-believe! The passerby on the streets pulling lizards out of their ears is so very scary scary scary! It's so scary that I'm going to swim away to some run-on sentence where everything is sweet & nice! But sweet & nice is the reason for crazy-musical-notes gushing everywhere you look! And we can do without our children hiding in the booty holes of giant monsters, can we?

Now here's the part where the words fall all over me! And what about the body parts of space aliens falling all over me too?! And of course, naughtiness is here to persuade us! And if the churning wheels of the machinery of our brains never stop then naughty-naughty happens! And if naughty-naughty happens, then – hey, what about the solar systems colliding with your head?? Have you thought about that? Or are you thinking about grabbing a jackhammer and crashing through outer space?

Lately I've been thinking about rearranging all the words in everybody's heads! But that's very Roman Empire in outer space! Especially

with all the Alice-in-Wonderland clones dancing

naked in the Old Testament! Because I just put

them there! But then again, there's always lots

of flying bullets to consider. And flying bullets

could wish you a happy day at any moment!

And then where would we be??

We would be in love with the sexy feet of

reptiles!"

The female vocalist begins singing a sexy-feet-

kind-of-song. The piano – however – is doing

lots of restless verbs. The saxophone is

spinning around in the universe of crack-

cocaine. And the drummer is dead from a

heroin overdose...

The monologue continues: "So whoops-ze-Daisy is so very very sexy with happy testicles on top! It's so very very talking bananas that naked Igor Stravinsky clones are running everywhere! Can you see the invisible words floating around us?? Because the space satellites are in love with our spermatozoa!

Instead, I'm seeing a bunch of lizards with huge teeth in front of me. And this audience of lizards is looking at me like they want to devour me! And that's not good! I mean, it's great! It's great with the actor on stage being devoured by the hungry audience! And that's why you all should devour all the angels in the sky with your giant teeth!

And what about all the gobs of humanity flooding out of these words?? And what about all the angry words leaping out of our stomachs?? And how shall we paint all these words everywhere??

What about that?"

The drummer is suddenly born-again as a Satanist, and the drummer begins playing a bunch of Satanic rebellions spreading across the Earth...

The monologue continues: "Now sometimes, the rocketships to Hell are very delicious with God's cum on top! Other times, so much gobbledygook is dripping from the ceilings of our brains! You know? You know??

Of course, rivers of sin want to baptize your naked flesh! Because too much testicles! Or is it my testicle insurance policy gone gazooks? Or maybe Mary Poppins is here to save us with her big plastic boobs?"

The saxophone plays so much zigzagging everything...

The monologue continues: "Now, tomorrow, I'm going to play music with a thousand decapitated heads! Or, am I going to fly into a painting and never come back? Or, perhaps I'll have sex with God?? Are you all going to dance with lots of rabies tomorrow?? Wouldn't that be great???

What's tomorrow going to look like anyway? Is lots of heavenly pornography going to happen tomorrow? Or is tomorrow going to be filled with so much fire? The fire of our flesh? The fire consuming our brains? Or will lots of sexy sheep singing erotic operas conquer tomorrow?"

The piano plays conquering tomorrow with lots of sexy mermaids.

The monologue continues: "I want to grab my own shit out of my anus, and paint great masterpieces with my own shit! I want to write the dialogues of plays with my own shit! I want to shake hands with friends with my own shit all over my hands!

My friends! Readers! Audience! Right now, let us reach our own hands up our butts – and reach in and grab our own shit – and smear our own shit all over each other's faces – as we recite the words of magic: 'Boomba-Zooooooooopa-Ooooooooppss!'

And if there's nobody next to you – if there's nobody around you – then smear your own shit all over your own face! And then walk outside, and let everybody see your own shit smeared all over your own face, as you tell all the passerby: 'Skiiieeeoooollllooppy! – Puuurrrrrrooooolllllooppyy! – Luuurrrroooollooopppyy!'"

And the female vocalist sings: "That's right! Skiiieeeoooollllooppy! – Puuurrrrrrooooollllooppyy! – Luuurrrroooollooopppyy!! That's all right!"

And the monologue continues: "The philosophy of scatology is going to save us! The religion of scatology is the Holy Kingdom of Doo-Doo! The whole human race has been waiting for the Holy Kingdom of Doo-Doo! Scatology is a tender answer to all the world's problems!

But what about losing your virginity to a grizzly bear on another planet?? And what about all the angels in heaven having sex with horny grizzly bears??"

The female vocalist sings: "Yes! What about all the little children floating up into outer space?? And what about having sex with all the wild animals that live downtown??"

The monologue man: "Yes! We must conquer all the quacking ducks on the moon! And we must sail our penises straight into the vaginas of other solar systems!"

The female vocalist: "Yes! Yes! Yes! We must stretch our tongues across outer space to eat that space alien vagina! And we must play the music of cunnilingus all day & night long!"

The monologue man: "And that's why the lions & tigers in our balls love to debate philosophy! And that's why we love to pour pussy juices all over our art!"

The female vocalist: "Yes to pouring pussy juices all over our art! And yes yes yes to discussing philosophy with lions & tigers as they eat us!"

The monologue man: "Can you see & taste the space alien jism dripping into this monologue??

Can you see & taste the strawberry mushroom clouds erupting everywhere??"

The female vocalist: "Yes yes yes! I can see the giant delicious strawberry of a mushroom cloud! I can see & taste the space-alien-jism dripping all over me!"

The monologue man: "Can the human race see all of this?? The human race must see the music painting everything into existence! Because of all the monsters erupting out of our heads! And all the angry nouns & sexy adjectives crawling out of the oceans!"

The female vocalist sings: "Because of all the angry nouns & sexy adjectives, the gods-in-the-sky will devour us! And all the children with hatchets in their hands will be chasing their parents down the streets!"

The monologue man: "And now it's time for a delicious cherry sauce all over our drive-by shootings!"

And the saxophone plays delicious cherry drive-by shootings.

The monologue man: "But before that, we must all repent for our jisms! We must repent for all our jisms by swallowing all the words in this monologue!"

The piano plays jisms! And the saxophone plays people swallowing all the words in this monologue...

The monologue man: "But before even that, we must all swim across an ocean of angry words! Yes! Yes! Yes!"

The female vocalist sings: "Yes! Yes! Yes!" while the drums are playing all the angry words in the ocean.

The monologue man: "Yes yes yes to all the zombies that want to eat us! Yes yes yes to all the cannibalism in our imaginations!"

The female vocalist sings: "Yes yes yes to all the chariots of madness! Chariots of madness whizzing us off to lots of sanity! Yes yes yes to all the animals in the rainforests joining us in our orgies of the bedroom!"

The monologue man: "Yes yes yes to painting the deliriums of our graffiti everywhere! And yes yes yes to re-creating our cities with the magic of the spraypaint cans in our hands!"

The female vocalist sings: "And yes yes yes to outer space adventures! And yes yes yes to frolicking in the imaginations of others! And yes yes yes to throwing all of our faces into the blender, and pouring the flesh all over the page!"

The monologue man: "The rampant colors of the words will save us! And the horny & hungry grizzly bears will save us too!"

The female vocalist sings: "But what about the teenage lust threatening us with underage immaculate conception?? And what about the birds & the bees crawling all over our skin??"

The monologue man: "The horny-hopping-kangaroos will happy us with horny new religions! And the sexy feet of the Virgin Mary will save us from the crazy craziness of preaching preachers!"

The female vocalist sings: "But you forgot about the pain in our thoughts! And you forgot about the thoughts that rot our insides every day!"

The monologue man: "Oh my laughing God-in-the-sky who's chanting George Carlin's seven forbidden words all day long! And I forgot about the herpes that makes us all so happy! And I forgot about the sunlight in our wet dreams! The monologue is ruined!"

The female vocalist sings: "The monologue is ruined! Ruined ruined ruined!!" And then the female vocalist makes a bunch of sad sounds. The saxophone plays manic craziness. The drums go into a manic-crazy-bravado! And the piano joins the drums in a breathless crescendo of everything manic & crazy!

The monologue man: "Somehow, I got the dolphins swimming in a toad's brains all wrong!

The female vocalist sings: "Somehow! Somehow! He got the lions & tigers devouring all the planets in the universe all wrong!"

Monologue man: "But I got the beautiful buttocks of English royalty all right!"

Female vocalist sings: "No he didn't! No he didn't!"

Monologue man: "What do you mean I didn't get the grasshoppers jumping all over the moon right?"

Female vocalist sings: "Because of the Herpes! Because of the lunatic asylums on other planets!"

Monologue man: "Because of the hordes-of-locusts flying out of the mouths of capitalist politicians? Because of the crazy-banana-people of our nightmares? But the electric chair is beautiful with evil! And this river of heroin is flowing through all the continents of the world!"

The female vocalist sings: "But this Armageddon of quacking ducks is from outer space! Did you think of that? Did you think of this maze of Leonardo da Vinci clones walking around Chicago's streets?? Huh? Huh?"

Monologue man: "Huh? Huh to the flying in-&-out of these words! And that's why I'm dancing with Josephine Baker for all eternity! You see! You see the walls & centuries & solar systems that they keep putting between you & me?!"

Female vocalist sings: "No I don't see no storm clouds in my pussy! And I don't see no spaceships flying off to the Republican Convention neither! So why don't you marry all those sheep on your farm? And why don't you eat a bowl full of nuclear armaments?"

The saxophone player plays a man eating a bowl of nuclear armaments...

The piano man plays a wedding ceremony of a man marrying all the sheep on his farm.

The drummer plays spaceships flying off to the Republican Convention...

Monologue man says: "You see? You see that? You see that Saturday night full of Queen of England whores on the street corner? And you see that Igor Stravinsky symphony chasing everybody down the street?"

The female vocalist sings: "Yes! I see that you have become King of that Giant Testicle floating in outer space! Yes! I see that there's too many crazy kangaroos hopping around in your studio apartment!"

Monologue man: "I said the planet Earth is made out of angry words blossoming everywhere!"

The female vocalist sings: "No you didn't! You said lots of space alien gobbledygook seasoned with the jizz of sex robots!"

Monologue man:
"Diiirrrreeeeeecccttooooorrrr!!"

The director walks on stage, as the saxophone plays billions of space aliens with giant mouths chewing up billions of human heads.

The director asks: "What's the problem now?"

The monologue man says: "It's the thousands of human babies crawling all over the stage here! It's the hot lava that keeps exploding out of the female vocalist's pussy!"

The female vocalist sings: "No! It's the thousands of army tanks that keep rolling all over the stage here! It's the zigzagging phrases of space-alien-languages that keep popping me upside the head!"

Somebody from the audience screams: "Hey! What about the sexy giraffes?! And what about the hooligans that were supposed to jump out of a giant cake and rape & kill everybody?"

The female vocalist sings: "Yeah! What about the sexy skyscrapers dressed up in French lingerie?! And what about the millions of humongous dandelions that were supposed to be growing out of the walls & the ceiling here!"

The saxophone plays all the capitalist politicians of the world having an orgy with billionaires...

The director screams: "I forgot to wear my underwear today!"

The monologue man says: "But what about the giant space alien that's stuck in my butthole? And what about the circus clowns that keep jumping into my head and laughing?"

The female vocalist sings: "And what about the monsters jumping out of the music and devouring us? And what about the dogs flying out of the clouds and peeing on us?"

An audience member screams: "And what about that river full of human eyeballs? And what about the words that jump out of our

mouths, even though we tell them not to?"

The director screams: "Where's that giant nose

that's supposed to fall out of outer space, and

crash onto the stage?!"

The saxophone plays hundreds of giant noses

falling out of the sky and crashing

everywhere...

The drummer plays his mother whipping him

when he was a child...

The piano plays everyone jumping from one

planet to the other...

The female vocalist sings: "When I was a child

I had hundreds of heads! And all my hundreds

of heads were always rolling down the hills of sanity! It was lots of fun!"

The director screams: "I want you all to pee on me right now! That's right! I want the entire cast & the entire audience to please pee on me now!"

An audience member screams: "Let's crash everything! Let's riot & riot until the world is ours! Let's riot & riot until poetry is as wide & open as the universe! I love you all!"

The saxophone plays everyone rioting...

The monologue man says: "I used to riot with all the animals on all the planets of the universe! It was lots of fun!"

The piano plays so much fun making our crotches itch...

The monologue man says: "I want to discover a thousand paintings behind every word! I want to walk on top of a delicious landscape of human flesh! I want to have sex with all the words in the dictionary!"

The drums play so many rabid orgies...

The monologue man says: "Where's my eternity filled with trippy words? And how come the endless cacophony of verbs & adjectives isn't here yet?!"

The director screams at the monologue man: "That's because you didn't fuck my wife like I told you to! Now jump on top of everybody's head, and dance & sing until Michelangelo is done painting you!"

An audience member screams at the director: "How come you love me so much?! And how come you didn't marry my dog and eat my cat?!"

The monologue man screams at the audience member: "Look, you! Why don't you go dancing in the ancient Roman Empire for a change?! And then you can lecture me about pussy eating!"

The female vocalist sings: "There's endless rooms full of sunshine in my brains! There's endless cannonballs blasting through all the serenity! Won't you create beautiful calligraphy with me?"

The saxophone plays the endless rooms full of sunshine...

The monologue man says: "I was dancing like a tornado inside all the endless rooms of sunshine inside her head! But then, the angels in the whorehouse called to me! And I drowned in a hurricane of naked flesh!"

An audience member says to the monologue man: "I want endless symphonies of crazy! I want endless diseases of sanity! I want so much catastrophe!"

The monologue man says to the audience member: "You masturbate with English aristocracy too much! You need to play the piano until flying saucers discover you! And then you should jump into Mother Teresa's vagina and stay there forever!"

The audience member answers: "Me?! But what about your diseases of the brains?! And you're always having a civil war with yourself!"

The monologue man answers: "You & me are like the planet Pluto & the planet Earth! We are like peasants rebelling against the gods! And that's why our words shall be victorious!"

The audience member answers: "The roller coaster of this moment is so stormy! I want to conquer all the art movements! I feel the sunshine turning my skin into sensuality!"

The saxophone plays a thousand years of sunshine & sensuality...

The monologue man answers: "The volcano of me will always be exploding! I will be exploding everything new! And I will be exploding everything musical! And then I will be exploding with everything in the future!"

The saxophone plays words skipping everywhere. The saxophone plays words frolicking in heaven. The saxophone plays words giggling & giggling...

An audience member yells: "I want confusion! I will attack! I will chop off my feet and give them to you!"

The female vocalist sings to the audience member: "Look to the oceans for your Satanic blessing! Look to the sky for your beautiful sins! And look to the hills & mountains for your worldly desires!"

The saxophone plays a crazy man escaping from an insane asylum...

The audience member answers the female vocalist: "I wish I could escape into millions of different minds! I want billions & billions of erotic sculptures hanging from the sky! I will destroy the heavens with my Penis!"

The saxophone plays brains boiling & boiling inside of heads...

The female vocalist sings to the audience member: "You must attack the peace & quiet with endless screaming poems! And then you can worship all the pagan idols in your Balzacs!

How will you all make your tomorrows drip with endless sensuality?"

And then the entire band plays the reader going insane! The entire band plays the audience going insane!

Monologue man says: "So much obscene graffiti to scream from my lungs! Too much censorship clogging up the floods of creativity! Not enough tidal waves of obscenity to wash away all the puritans!"

The director: "The end of the play is here. Please take these words from this monologue away with you, and plant the seeds of obscenity everywhere!"

The female vocalist: "Remember! Plant those seeds of obscenity! Let obscenity blossom in the arts and in the human race and in our future! Let the erotic Garden of Eden grow all around us!"

The saxophone plays the erotic Garden of Eden growing everywhere...

www.ingramcontent.com/pod-product-compliance
Lightning Source LLC
Chambersburg PA
CBHW071228090426
42736CB00014B/3007